MW01531813

First in Their Hearts

First in Their Hearts

Early Biographers
of
George Washington

Weems, Marshall, Sparks, Irving

Gerard M. Cataldo

&

Barbara L. H. Chesney

CHESTER RIVER PRESS
2011

Design by James Dissette

ISBN: 970-0-9833269-0-2

Copyright @ 2011 Gerard Cataldo
Copyright © 2011 Barbara Chesney

SECOND PRINTING

CHESTER RIVER PRESS
Chestertown. Maryland
www.chesterriverpress.com

Introduction

The presentations in this volume by Gerard M. Cataldo and Barbara L. H. Chesney were delivered to the Old Kent Chapter of the Daughters of the American Revolution on February 10, 2011, in Chestertown, Maryland. The presentations were in honor of the birthday of George Washington, in the spirit of the NSDAR mission of promoting historic preservation, education, and patriotism.

Gerard Cataldo is a rare book dealer, writer and publisher, and Barbara Chesney is an educator, member of the Old Kent Chapter, and a descendant by marriage of Mason Locke Weems.

"...first in war, first in peace, and first in the hearts of his countrymen."

General Henry Lee,
eulogy for George Washington

Contents

Four Early Biographers of George Washington

Gerard M. Cataldo

In 1797, America was facing a transition as uncertain as the periods from 1775 to 1783, and from 1787 to 1797. The Continental Congress appointed George Washington as commander-in-chief of the Continental Army in 1775, beginning an eight year war for independence, the success of which was never a foregone conclusion. In 1787, Washington presided over the Philadelphia Convention which drafted the Constitution, leading to a ten year period wherein the Constitution was ratified and Washington was elected president and served until 1797. Now the republic faced a future without Washington, a transfer of political power and leadership for the first time to a new president and administration. The great George Washington was now relegated to history, no longer the visible, stalwart image of the United States.

And who was Washington? Did the American public share a uniform opinion of the military leader and first president, or was the image clouded by the politics of the moment, the controversies of his second term, the Jeffersonian distrust of his Federalist philosophies, or the ire over the Jay Treaty with Britain? Such were the questions to be left to historians, the facts and narrative of a public life which would need to be handed down and presented to his people and finally to posterity. Each nation is judged by its written history, presented with all the biases and opinions of any human endeavor. But the desire for icons, those statues-in-print of prophets, kings, queens, Caesars, and presidents, demands that the historians and biographers take up their pens and present the great men and women of their time to their subjects. America was a young nation, and as such it became even more urgent to enshrine their "Founding Father" on the high altar of history.

In order to know who we are, we need to know who our leaders are. The United States was not founded on birthright, ethnicity, religion, ancient maps, language, or a two thousand year old history of legend, myth, and deeds. The nation was founded on ideas, beliefs, values, and a vision of a political and governmental system different from and more libertarian than the system from which it emerged. It is no wonder then, that we Americans hold our founders in such awe. They were not born into their positions, rather they took up arms, declared independence, wrote constitutions, debated rights and freedoms, and amazingly, despite the political intrigues and maneuverings of their time, managed to place high minded principles above petty bickering. To understand the magnitude of their accomplishments, young America sought, and we continue to seek, a clearer understanding of who the founders really were.

It has been said that myth is the seed of history. We should not be surprised therefore, that the first biographer of George Washington, Mason Locke Weems, saw his duty in 1799 as establishing the first president as an icon of American greatness. In his pamphlet entitled *The Life and Memorable Actions of George Washington*, Weems' reliance on the personal attributes of Washington, surmised or actual, is consistent with the common perception that the individual values and qualities of the founders had the most profound effect on the eventual establishment of our national ideals. That Washington was a man of high character has not been seriously debated. He was subjected to political opposition, especially during his second term in office, but throughout the revolutionary war and his assent to the presidency he was perceived as a reluctant hero who placed duty and country above his personal comfort.

Critics will contend that in placing excessive emphasis on personal qualities, and in fact taking liberties with anecdotal statements of his life, Weems elevated Washington to demigod status, thus obfuscating his human and political frailties. While there is certainly some truth to that observation, we should remember that Weems was astute enough to recognize that America sought confirmation of its chosen path in the intentions and high mindedness of its leaders, George Washington in particular.

Weems' eighty page booklet, later expanded in 1808 to the two hundred page biography with the lengthy title *The Life of Washington with Curious Anecdotes Equally Honorable to Himself and Exemplary to his Young Countrymen,* continues to hold the interest of the reading public. In 1962 The Belknap Press of Harvard University Press issued a republication of Weems' *The Life of Washington,* based on the 1809 ninth edition, as part of the Loeb Classical Library Series. That publication is now in its twelfth printing.

During the period when Weems was attempting to find a publisher for his biography, Chief Justice John Marshall, at the request of Washington's nephew Bushrod Washington, began to plan his own multi-volume *Life of Washington.* Bushrod Washington possessed original materials written by and to George Washington and promised their use to Marshall in the writing of the biography. Marshall was eager to undertake the project for two reasons: his admiration for George Washington, and his need for compensation to supplement his salary and the income from his land holdings. In discussing the project, Marshall and Bushrod Washington were optimistic concerning the prospective sales of the biography and the royalties they would both receive.

Eventually published in 1807 in five volumes, Marshall's work would become a much anticipated and subsequently much criticized attempt to recount the history of the continent and the nation within the framework of George Washington's life. Marshall's approach was extensive, some would say ponderous, lacking a clear perception of the interests of the public. Because Marshall served with Washington in the military and knew him on a personal level, the expectations for the work were high, only to be dashed by the first volume which dealt with early history, the voyages of exploration, and the colonial settlements, mentioning Washington only briefly toward the end.

To Marshall's credit, he grasped the reality of the mediocre reception of his work, and spent time revising and restructuring his approach to the biography. In the end his best writing covered the Revolutionary War period in volumes three and four, which were received with praise and relief by the public. Marshall was not without controversy, as his writing became entangled in the political issues of the day, attracting criticism from Jefferson and the Republicans that the biography was a Federalist manifesto.

In the end Marshall was never satisfied with his work, and his desire to publish a revised edition of his *Life of Washington* was realized in 1832. He removed the infamous first volume, subsequently publishing it separately in 1842 as a *History of the Colonies*. Marshall prided himself on the fact that he had researched Washington's personal correspondence and papers in preparation for his biography. In fact he and Bushrod Washington had planned a three volume edition of Washington's correspondence from the Revolutionary War period.

In 1824, Charles Folsom, a Boston printer, contacted the historian Jared Sparks and proposed that he publish a complete edition of Washington's writings. Through extensive negotiations with Bushrod Washington and John Marshall, Sparks was granted access to the full trove of Washington's writings in storage at Mount Vernon. In March of 1827 Sparks arrived at Mt. Vernon to begin his research. He spent a month reviewing the material and planning his approach to the sorting, editing and presentation of the documents, which included diaries, forty thousand letters, notebooks, and hundreds of scraps of writings and notes. Sparks concluded it would take a year just to read through the documents, and with Bushrod's permission, made arrangements to box and ship all of the papers to Boston, where he commenced work arranging the documents chronologically and editing the contents. He subsequently moved to Cambridge into the Craigie House, where George Washington had lived and worked when he took command of the American Army.

It was the beginning of a ten year project that would be mired in controversy. Sparks had previously researched and published the correspondence and papers of Gouverneur Morris, John Ledyard, and Benjamin Franklin, and in 1829 published *The Diplomatic Correspondence of the American Revolution* in twelve volumes. Early on Sparks decided that the publication of Washington's papers should be accompanied by a new "Life of Washington," which would paint an accurate picture of Washington based on important information he would find in the archives.

Well aware of the disappointing reception of Marshall's work, Sparks elected to devote a single volume to Washington's life, staying clear of the political intrigue that was associated with Marshall. His biography is a straightforward account, interjecting new facts and interpretations, and written with an eye toward satisfying the reading public with a relatively concise biography of the "Founding Father." The text is heavily complimentary to Washington in retelling his private, military, and public life. Sparks presented Washington adorned with the confidence and loyalty of the people. When describing the deliberations concerning the choice for first president, he writes: "It was no sooner ascertained, that the constitution would probably be adopted, than the eyes of the nation were turned upon Washington, as the individual to be selected for that office...the interest in the subject, therefore, was intense...."

The work was completed in one volume in 1837, and became Volume I of the twelve volumes of *The Life and Writings of George Washington*. The biography was published separately in 1838, and shortly after in 1839, in two volumes, the so-called abridged edition. The biography was well received and brought praise from Marshall, George Bancroft, Edward Everett, and William Prescott. Typical of the comments was this by Bancroft: "...it is saying little to say your book should be in every American family; you have been first to give the world a full length portrait of Washington, and I set the highest value alike on your larger picture and on this its miniature."

The criticism of Sparks' larger work, *The Writings of George Washington*, centered on the editorial license he had taken with the prose of Washington's letters, which Sparks altered to conform to more acceptable grammar and style, and his rephrasing of certain descriptive writings concerning prominent individuals or events. Sparks justified his work by stating that Washington's writings were private, not intended for public exposure, and that in the interest of the "dignity of history" he would not have wanted them exposed without correction. Even so, the controversy continues, and is referenced today when similar license is taken with the release of private papers of prominent individuals.

Washington Irving was born in New York on April 3, 1783, the week of the British cease fire that ended the Revolutionary War. His mother named him after George Washington, whom he met at the age of six in New York after Washington's inauguration as president in 1789. In the same year, due to an outbreak of yellow fever in Manhattan, he was sent to live with friends at Tarrytown in upstate New York. It was there he was exposed to local Dutch culture, legends, ghost stories, Sleepy Hollow, and the Catskills. He began writing in earnest at the age of nineteen, submitting commentaries to newspapers under the name Jonathan Oldstyle, the first of many pseudonyms he would use. He travelled to Europe in 1804, financed by his brothers, and on his return two years later collaborated on publishing a literary magazine, *Salmagundi*, in which he first used the nickname "Gotham" for New York City. In 1809 he completed work on his first book *A History of New York from the Beginning of the World to the End of the Dutch Dynasty*, under the pseudonym Diedrich Knickerbocker, purportedly a Dutch historian, whose name became identified as a nickname for New Yorkers.

Washington Irving's career was both literary and political. He spent many years in Europe, where he wrote *The Sketch Book of Geoffrey Crayon, Gent., The Life and Voyages of Christopher Columbus, The Chronicles of the Conquest of Granada*, and *Voyages and Discoveries of the Companions of Columbus*, as well as serving as Secretary to the American Legation in London. In 1846, Irving returned to Tarrytown, New York after spending four years as United States Minister to Spain. Irving's habit was to work on several writing projects simultaneously, and he undertook a project proposed by the publisher George Putnam to work on a revised new edition of his complete works. He had begun preliminary work on a *Life of George Washington*, which he envisioned as a three volume biography, and he now decided it was time to devote his remaining years to researching and writing the biography in earnest.

Irving hired his nephew Pierre as a full time assistant on the project, and planned the biography as a thorough narrative history, referencing the latest writings and documents, including Sparks' publication of Washington's correspondence. Irving was of the belief that an accurate biography of Washington should focus on the public man, and that the story of America's independence and nationhood was indistinguishable from that of Washington, "the principal actor." Aware of the criticisms of the writing techniques of both Sparks and Marshall, Irving approached the biography of Washington as a professional writer, taking particular care with style and readability. Further, being aware of the pedestal upon which Washington rested, he would protect his subject from full exposure, refraining from anecdotes relating to Washington's alleged petulance and irritability.

The result was a well-researched, accessible biography that conforms to the established complimentary story of a man of morals and unselfish commitment. Early in 1855 Putnam released the first volume of Irving's *Life of George Washington*, which covered the period up to the American Revolution. By Christmas volume two was ready for publication, covering the beginning of the Revolution, containing detailed descriptions of battles and Washington's military leadership. As with the first volume, the second was highly praised, with Prescott writing that it portrayed Washington as a "flesh and blood" figure, and "one with whom we can have sympathy."

The third volume of Irving's *Washington* was published in July of 1856, and covered the period from the encampment at Morristown to Washington's fortification of West Point. This volume is prefaced by Irving: "When the author commenced the publication of this work, he informed the publishers that he should probably complete it in three volumes...his theme has unexpectedly expanded under his pen, and now he lays his third volume before the public, with his task yet unaccomplished...." In fact it took all of volume four, published in May 1857, to close out his narrative of the Revolution, ending with Washington's election to the presidency and the inauguration. Volume five, the last, was published in 1859, to which Irving prefaced: "The present volume completes a work to which the author had long looked forward as the crowning effort of his literary career...he resigns his last volume to its fate...." The generous accolades for Irving's completed work attested to Irving's high standing in literary America, and to the copious research and popular narrative style of the biography. *The Life of George Washington* would be Irving's last work. He died in November of 1859 at the age of 76.

As this overview of the early biographers of George Washington attests, America's fascination with its first president continued unabated through the early years of the nation. As is evident from the hundreds of books, essays, articles, pamphlets and media profiles of Washington in the years since then, our interest in the principal figure of our national history endures. This is an understandable phenomenon, since as stated in the beginning, in order to know and understand who we are today, we need to know who our founders were. Whether written in the form of myth, gospel, anecdote, or fact, these portraits of Washington stand as testament to our curiosity and introspection. Biographers reveal as much about the reading public as they do their subjects. That these biographies have endured through the history of the nation is a tribute to the writers and to us all.

Thomas Carlyle wrote that biography is the only true history, and by extension, biographers are the true historians. Here in the year 2011 still another biography of Washington has been published, *Washington a Life*, by Ron Chernow. Initial reviews are positive and in fact complimentary. And so 235 years after our Declaration of Independence, we continue to seek answers, inspiration, and purpose from the life of George Washington, a unique man, who deservedly remains... first in our hearts.

Undeniably Great
George Washington as Viewed by Mason Locke Weems

Barbara L. H. Chesney

George Washington's first biographer was Mason Locke Weems, who was born in Anne Arundel County, Maryland, October 1, 1759. His family came to the western shore of Maryland from Weemshire on the eastern shore of Scotland. The land in Scotland had been given to MacDuff, Thane of Fife, who slew Macbeth in 1057. MacDuff became know as MacDuff Weems, named after the coves, caves, and inlets along the coast of Weemshire.

The Weems family carried this name to America. In 1720, David Weems, his mother, Lady Elizabeth Loch Weems, his brother, James, and his sister, Williamina, ventured to Anne Arundel County, Maryland, to live with Dr. William Loch, the brother of Lady Elizabeth Loch Weems. Dr. William Loch, owned large estates located between Herring Bay and West River on the Chesapeake Bay. Land records of Anne Arundel County show that in 1733, David purchased 150 acres of land called "Marches Seat" on Herring Creek. He was a tobacco farmer, but he also was a Privateer. He invested with others as a patriot-owner of two privateer ships, the schooner Williamanta and the sloop Washington. As such, he held a government commission to intercept enemy merchant ships. He also served on the vestry of Saint James Episcopal Church, Herring Creek, and helped with its construction and development.

David married twice and had 19 children, five of whom died in infancy. His youngest child was Mason Locke Weems, who inherited David's "Negro Boy Mead." Mason Locke Weems later gave Mead his freedom.

As a young boy, Weems was sent to Kent Free School in Chestertown, Maryland, on the Eastern Shore of the Chesapeake Bay. Kent Free School was a boarding school that became Washington College. Weems studied medicine, and in 1784 he became one of the first two persons ordained by the Church of England for ministry in the United States. He returned to this country without having to pledge allegiance to the King of England due to an act passed by the English Parliament. Upon his return to the United States, he worked as an itinerant preacher, traveling from church to church. As he traveled, he sold Bibles and other books for the nation's leading publisher, Mathew Carey of Philadelphia.

Parson Weems sold books for Mathew Carey to augment his meager wages as an itinerant preacher, and he was considered to be one of the best salesmen that the company had. He felt that the selling of "good books" was a field for God's work. As a minister, he was familiar with the Bible and its method of communicating with parables and stories, and he realized that he would make more money if he wrote the books that he was selling. Therefore, he began to write, using a format similar to the format of the Bible. In 1800, he published an eighty-page pamphlet entitled *The Life and Memorable Actions of George Washington.* Parson Weems revised the biography every year until he died on May 23, 1825. As the book was revised, the title changed which explains why the biography is known by several names. It continues to be reprinted today, and has been a popular book for over two hundred years.

The edition that was published in 1806 is referred to as the "fifth edition" because the first edition was not widely distributed. The fifth edition included the stories, or myths, about George Washington that are so well known. In presenting them, Parson Weems stated that he had heard them from others and that he was using them to illustrate virtues and moral truths. It is said that George Washington, upon hearing these tales, never indicated whether or not they were true. A mystique, therefore, grew around the personality traits of George Washington, making him more venerated and more loved than he had been.

Mason Locke Weems considered himself the rector of "Mount-Vernon Parish." George Washington and his father worshiped at Pohick Church near Dumfries, Virginia, where Mason Locke Weems and his wife, Frances Ewell, established their household. Family oral history reveals that the tale of the cherry tree was created by Parson Weems one Sunday morning as he delivered a sermon on honesty. He often used stories that focused on morals and values in his sermons, and on one particular Sunday morning, Parson Weems noticed George Washington sitting in the front pew. He wanted to signal to the rest of the congregation that such an important person was in their midst. Therefore, he created the story of young George chopping down the cherry tree and being confronted by his father to illustrate the virtue of honesty.

Parson Weems also had ample opportunity to observe George Washington at family gatherings. Parson Weems' wife, Frances Ewell, traced her heritage to the Ball family as did George's mother, Mary Ball Washington. Parson Weems wished to elevate George Washington and to show that he was indeed as great a man in private life as he was in public life. Weems wrote, "It is not in the glare of public, but in the shade of private life, that we are to look for the man. Private life, is always real life. Behind the curtain, where the eyes of the million are not upon him, and where a man can have no motive but inclination, no incitement but honest nature, there he will always be sure to act himself; consequently, if he act greatly, he must be great indeed. Hence it has been justly said, that our private deeds, if noble, are noblest of our lives."

To portray George Washington as a "real" person in his private life and to elevate the very public figure who possessed the virtues desired by everyone, Weems discussed the milestones of the life of George Washington as well as the development of his character. His upbringing was woven throughout the book, and whole chapters were devoted to his general character and to specific traits such as benevolence, industry, and patriotism.

The final chapter, which focused on the patriotism of Washington, likened him to iconic world leaders such as the Roman Emperor

Alexander and British Admiral Blake. Comments about the noble spirit of Washington gave way to rousing passages that suggested fellow countrymen carry on what the Founding Fathers had begun. A mixture of religious prose and patriotic encouragement combined in a way that it revealed Mason Locke Weems as an ardent motivational writer. He encouraged all to summon the spirit of '76, to respect their country, to comply with her laws, and to serve her well.

In ending the biography, Parson Weems gave a final blessing, which closely resembled "George Washington's Prayer For Our Country." The first President of the new nation offered this prayer in a private service at Saint Paul's Church after his brief inaugural address to Congress. Mason Locke Weems used it in his book as a blessing and as a way of encouraging others to hold themselves up to the high ideals of George Washington. In the end, the myth-maker and the person about whom the myths were created merged and became one. The likeable, eloquent, and entertaining author led his readers to the point of striving to be as virtuous as George Washington, whose life and memorable actions sought the common good.

Truly, Mason Locke Weems was a man of undeniable character as was George Washington. Mason Locke Weems was an itinerant minister, a traveling book salesman, a student and a teacher of the Bible, an educator who understood how the Bible taught its lessons, an analyst of human nature, a motivator, an entertainer, and a citizen who loved, admired, and elevated the first President of our country. He was a complex individual who set out to make a mark, and he did it with persistence, focused attention, and many advantages. He was born into an aristocratic family that held titles, land, and positions, he was a relative of George Washington, he was trained and educated, and he was motivated to succeed. He sought stories, he made up stories, he stretched the truth, he found the truth. He searched far and wide, all with a likeable quality that gave the people what they wanted and what he felt they needed. And, he made George Washington first in their hearts.

Vignettes of the Biographers

by Gerard M. Cataldo

Mason Locke Weems
(10/11/1756 — 5/23/1825)

The Life and Memorable Actions of George Washington, by Mason Locke Weems (published anonymously)1800.

The Life of George Washington with Curious Anecdotes Equally Honorable to Himself and Exemplary to his Young Countrymen, by Mason Locke Weems. Philadelphia: Matthew Carey, 1808.

Mason Locke Weems, commonly known as Parson Weems, was born October 11, 1759 in Anne Arundel County, Maryland. He studied theology in England and was ordained in 1784. Returning to Maryland he served in that capacity until 1790 when he became a book agent for Philadelphia publisher Matthew Carey. He became a well-known and successful travelling book salesman, his method being to attend public events, pitch his books, interject humorous anecdotes, play his violin, and preach salvation and temperance distributing his own pamphlet entitled "Drunkards Glass."

In June of 1799 Weems informed Carey that he had begun to write a biography of George Washington, to which he attached various titles including *A History of the Life and Death, Virtues and Exploits of General George Washington*, and *The True Patriot, or Beauties of Washington ...abundantly biographical and anecdotal curious and marvelous.* By October he had completed an eighty page booklet and urged Carey to publish it immediately as the public was desirous of a biography of the man Weems called "the greatest man that ever lived." While Carey pondered the decision to publish Weems, the author arranged to have the booklet printed himself, and by 1800, after Washington's death, four printings had appeared and sold successfully.

Weems was engaged by Carey to help sell Marshall's biography of Washington, and after the lukewarm reception of Marshall's first volume Weems repeatedly urged Carey to terminate the Marshall project and publish his biography. By 1806 Weems had revised his booklet, providing new anecdotes and "facts." In 1807, after the completion of Marshall's biography, Weems expanded his booklet into 200 pages, and Carey published it in 1808 under the title *The Life of Washington with Curious Anecdotes Equally Honorable to Himself and Exemplary to his Young Countrymen*, sixth edition. This publication was reissued twenty times before Weems' death in 1825. It sold at ten-times the pace of Marshall's work.

Weems' biography concentrates on the virtues of Washington, capitalizing on the esteem in which the public held the first president. It has been said that the biography could have been titled "The Gospel of George Washington, according to Mason Locke Weems," and indeed the structure of the work is based on parables, anecdotes, and the personal virtues attributed to Washington. The mythology contained in Weems' work has had a longstanding effect on the attitudes of Americans concerning Washington, and many of the stories Weems offers, such as the over-commented on "Cherry Tree Story" survive today as being examples of virtues to strive for and admire.

For all its dubious claims for Washington, Weems' popular biography set the reverential tone for all the biographies which followed. Marshall, Sparks, and Irving concentrated on the public Washington with an eye towards a chronological and factual retelling, albeit tinged with personal and political biases, but none strayed from a complimentary portrait. Weems focused on the man, his legend, his grandiosity, and his personal virtues. To Weems, Washington was the icon to which all others would be compared. He understood the young Republic's yearning for heroes, the search for greatness in its leaders. He sculpted a portrait that filled that need, and in so doing transcended any criticism directed at his work.

John Marshall
(9/24/1755 — 7/6/1835)

*The Life of George Washington, Commander in Chief of the American
Forces, during the War which established the Independence of his Country,
and First President of the United States, Compiled under the Inspection
of the Honourable Bushrod Washington, from Original Papers...To which
is prefixed a compendious view of the Colonies planted by the English on
the Continent of North America.* by John Marshall. Philadelphia: C.P.
Wayne, 1804-1807, 5 vols.

John Marshall was born in 1755, in Germantown, at what is now
Fauquier County in Virginia. He attended Campbell Academy in
Washington Parish, and continued his studies under the supervision
of his father, who provided him with a copy of Blackstone's *Commentaries on the Laws of England.* He served in the Continental Army during the Revolutionary War, and was a friend of George Washington.
Subsequently he read law at the College of William and Mary, and
was admitted to the Bar in 1780.

In 1782 Marshall was elected to the Virginia House of Delegates,
served on the Council of State, and became Recorder of the Richmond City Hustings Court. In 1788 he was selected as a delegate to
the Virginia convention on the United States Constitution, where
along with James Madison and Edmund Randolph, he supported rati-
fication. Marshall favored the Federalist Party, which identified with
a strong national government, as opposed to the Jeffersonian Demo-
cratic-Republican Party, which strongly advocated states' rights.

In 1801 President John Adams appointed several federal judges during the last weeks of his presidential term. Among the appointments was John Marshall as Chief Justice of the United States.

Not long after the death of George Washington in 1799, Washington's nephew Bushrod Washington discussed with Marshall a project to become Washington's biographer. Bushrod Washington possessed original materials written by and to George Washington and promised their use to Marshall in the writing of the biography. Marshall was eager to undertake the project for two reasons: his admiration for George Washington, and his need for compensation to supplement his salary and the income from his land holdings. In discussing the project, Marshall and Bushrod Washington were optimistic concerning the prospective sales of the biography and the royalties they would both receive.

It took two years of negotiation with printers before Bushrod Washington and Marshall signed a contract with C.P. Wayne, a Philadelphia publisher. They decided the biography would comprise four or five volumes, with thirty thousand subscribers, and agreed to accept $100,000 for the United States copyright. Wayne argued that the most ever paid for copyright of one work was $30,000, and pointed out that the highest subscriber rate for any previous work had been two thousand. An agreement was signed in 1802, with the work projected as being four or five volumes, octavo in size, from four to five hundred pages each, and completed in two years.

As word began to circulate that a massive biography of George Washington was in the planning stages, Marshall tried to conceal the fact that he was to be the author. However, President Jefferson soon got wind of the project, and began an effort to discredit the biography on the grounds that it would be an anti-Jefferson, anti-Republican book, designed to influence the outcome of the next election. He persisted in these efforts to condemn the biography throughout the entire publishing process. Using the powers of his office, Jefferson thwarted Wayne's efforts to secure subscribers for the work by pressuring the Post Masters to limit the sales.

Wayne engaged book agents in the effort to secure subscribers, among them Mason Locke Weems, whose own booklet biography of Washington had been published in 1800. Weems discovered that

Jefferson's efforts were bearing fruit in that apprehension about Marshall's project was growing, most notably in New England, even before a manuscript had been finished and sent to the publisher. Weems passed along these concerns to Wayne, who had already received demands from early subscribers for refunds.

Finally, three years after deciding to write the biography, Marshall finished the manuscript for the first volume. It was a massive piece of writing, which Wayne declared would require 800 pages in print, thus increasing costs. To add to the publisher's woes, Marshall insisted again that his name not be placed on the title page of the volume. Wayne forcefully argued against Marshall's wishes, and Marshall acquiesced with the caveat that his association with the Supreme Court not be mentioned. Marshall was completing his draft of the second volume when the proof sheets of volume one were returned to him for review. He was shocked by the errors and inaccuracies, and by the sheer length of the first volume. Further, in the entire first volume, George Washington's name was only mentioned twice toward the end of the book. The volume covered the early history of the continent from the voyages of discovery, through the exploration and settlement of America, to the history of the Colonies up to 1765. Marshall decided to retitle the first volume as an Introduction to the *Life of Washington*.

Marshall took pains to prevent errors and reduce the length of volume two, but when he received the proofs for the second volume discovered the carelessness of his writing. He informed Wayne that the first two volumes would need to be revised before a second edition could ever be published.

In the summer of 1804 the first two volumes were published, with dismal reception. Marshall devoted just one page at the beginning of volume two to the ancestry, birth, and development of Washington to age nineteen. He hastily covered Washington's experience in the French and Indian Wars, and repeated a description of Braddock's defeat from volume one. Marshall described the debates over the Declaration of Independence in less than two pages. Volume two is strong on military matters, but weak on the involvement of Washington in the political and formative issues of the nation. Marshall reacted to the criticism by realizing that he misjudged the appetite of the public for a long treatise on the development of the continent, and should have concentrated instead on the early life of Washington and the beginning of his military career. The financial ramifications of the unpopularity of the initial volumes were pressing on Marshall and the publisher. With the subscriber list dwindling, Wayne sought to change the publishing contract with Bushrod Washington and Marshall. Only two copies had been sold to non-subscribers.

By 1805 Marshall's third volume was published, and was a vast improvement on the first two. Volume three covered the Revolutionary War to 1779, containing satisfactory descriptions of the battles of Brandywine, Germantown, and Monmouth, each of which he participated in. But his description of Valley Forge was criticized as being neither comprehensive nor vivid.

The more Marshall wrote, however, the clearer and more precise he became. Volume four, suffering less criticism that the previous three volumes, contained an admired recounting of the treason of Benedict Arnold, and an accurate analysis of the formulation of political parties as the Revolutionary War came to a close. The fourth volume ends with Washington's farewell to his officers, and his military retirement.

By 1807 Marshall had completed his fifth and final volume, which dealt with Washington's nationalism, the foundation of political parties, the union, the Articles of Confederation, and the disputes between America and Great Britain over the Treaty of Peace. His description of the Constitutional Convention was criticized as having omitted Washington's influence on the deliberations, and for the lack of discussion of *The Federalist*. He recounts the pressures placed on Washington to become President, but allots more writing to the various appeals on Washington than he does on the deliberations on the Constitution. He took twenty pages to describe Washington's travels to New York for his inauguration, but was frustratingly brief on his election to the Presidency.

Many critics of the period applauded Marshall's coverage of the effect of the French Revolution on the United States, and the hostility to Washington's *Proclamation of Neutrality*. In the final volume Marshall presents Washington's *Farewell Address* in full, and describes Washington's illness and death. Several observers lauded the final volume as being "worth all the rest."

For the rest of his life Marshall pored over the biography, making revisions and corrections. His desire was to reissue the biography in a new edition, and in 1832 a revised biography was published. Marshall retitled the first volume as *History of the American Colonies* (published separately in 1824 as *A History of the Colonies Planted by the English on the Continent of North America, from their Settlement, to the Commencement of the War, which terminated in their Independence,* Philadelphia, Abraham Small, 1824) and the remaining four volumes were reduced to two, albeit two large volumes. But according to most critics, the revised version was a vast improvement over the original, leading many to speculate that the initial reception of the work would have been more favorable, and lucrative, had proper revisions been accomplished prior to original publication. During the period Marshall wrote his *Life of Washington,* he wrote fifty-six opinions in cases decided in the Circuit Court in Richmond, and twenty-seven decided by the Supreme Court, including *Marbury vs. Madison.*

Jared Sparks
(5/10/1789 — 3/14/1866)

The Life of George Washington, by Jared Sparks. Boston: Ferdinand Andrews, 1839.

Jared Sparks was born in Willington, Connecticut, on May 10, 1789. He attended Phillips Exeter Academy from 1809-1811, graduated from Harvard in 1815, studied Theology at the Harvard Divinity School and was a Unitarian Minister from 1819 to 1829, being the Chaplain of the U.S. House of Representatives from 1821 to 1823. Sparks was owner and editor of the *North American Review,* the first literary magazine in the United States. Sparks was elected president of Harvard in 1849, serving in that capacity until 1853. Jared Sparks' historical research and writings justifies his reputation as one of the preeminent historians and men of letters in early America. His accomplishments include:

The Life of John Ledyard, the American Traveller, Comprising Selections from His Journals and Correspondence, 1828. Ledyard was an explorer who lived among the Iroquois, and travelled with Captain James Cook on his last voyage around the world.

The Diplomatic Correspondence of the American Revolution, 1829. A twelve volume work containing letters of prominent men of the Revolution, including Franklin, Adams, and Jay.

The Life of Gouverneur Morris, with Selections from his Correspondence and Miscellaneous Papers, 1832, three volumes.

A Collection of the Familiar Letters and Miscellaneous Papers of Benjamin Franklin, 1833.

The Writings of George Washington, 1834. Considered Sparks' premier work, twelve volumes of Washington's papers and correspondence, with Volume One being a *Life of Washington,* which was actually written last and completed in 1837.

The Works of Benjamin Franklin, with Notes and a Life of the Author, 1836-1840, ten volumes.

Correspondence of the American Revolution..., 1853. His final historical work, contains correspondence from nearly 200 writers of the period, four volumes.

The idea to publish the correspondence of George Washington was first proposed to Sparks in March, 1824, by Charles Folsom, then connected with a printing house in Cambridge. Folsom wanted to publish a complete edition of Washington's writings. Sparks began a communication with Bushrod Washington, the nephew of George Washington and a Justice of the Supreme Court, concerning access to the writings and correspondence. Judge Washington had been working with John Marshall, Chief Justice of the United States, whose five volume biography of Washington was published in 1804-1807, and who had already commenced editing on a project to publish three volumes of Washington's letters written during the Revolutionary War period. Judge Washington essentially refused to grant permission for Sparks to access the complete correspondence at Mount Vernon. Sparks was not to be denied, however, and set out on his own to gather and review correspondence located in the public offices of several Southern and Middle states, contacting governors and other officials for access. By 1826 Sparks had reviewed and made notes on a large body of correspondence, and set out on a tour of the New England states for the same purpose.

Sparks, deciding he was in a much stronger position to be granted access to the Mount Vernon documents than he previously was, petitioned Judge Washington again, informing him of the progress he had made on his own. In a written proposal, Sparks offered to divide the property of the copyright and profits from the sale of a publication equally with the Judge, additionally granting him the right to withhold any document he deemed not suited for publication. Sparks wrote to Marshall explaining the proposition, and received replies within days of each other from Marshall and Washington accepting the proposal.

In March of 1827 Sparks arrived at Mt. Vernon to begin his research. He spent a month reviewing the material and planning his approach to the sorting, editing and presentation of the documents, which included diaries, forty thousand letters, notebooks, and hundreds of scraps of writings and notes. Sparks concluded it would take a year just to read through the documents, and with the Judge's permission, made arrangements to box and ship all of the papers to Boston, where he commenced work arranging the documents chronologically and editing the contents. He subsequently moved to Cambridge into the Craigie House, where George Washington had lived and worked when he took command of the American Army.

Sparks decided that the publication of Washington's correspondence should be accompanied by a "Life of Washington." He felt that the documents in his possession provided important additional information which would paint a more accurate portrait of Washington than had been accomplished earlier, particularly by Marshall. He set out planning a chronological narrative of Washington's life, which was completed in nineteen chapters with an appendix containing the Rules of Behavior, Expenses as Commander-in-chief of the American Armies, and the Farewell Address. Sparks devoted seven chapters of the "Life" to Washington's military affairs, and four chapters to his presidency and the immediate aftermath.

Well aware of the poor reception of Marshall's biography of Washington, Sparks elected to devote a single volume to his biography, and stayed clear of the political intrigues and perceptions of party bias that had plagued Marshall. His biography is a straightforward account, interjecting new facts and interpretations gleaned from his painstaking perusal of the correspondence and writings. But Sparks, being an editor and literary figure, was attuned to what the reading public expected and desired in a biography of the father of the country. Accordingly, the text is heavily complimentary to Washington in retelling his private, military, and public life. Sparks presented his subject adorned with the confidence and loyalty of the people, as when discussing the deliberations on who the first president should be, he writes: "It was no sooner ascertained, that the constitution would probably be adopted, than the eyes of the nation were turned upon Washington, as the individual to be selected for that office [President of the United States] the highest, most honorable, and most responsible, that could be conferred by the suffrages of a free people...In him whole people would be united...The interest felt in the subject, therefore, was intense; and at no period, even during the struggle of the revolution, was the strong support of Washington more necessary, than at this crisis."

The work was completed in one volume in 1837, and became Volume I of the twelve volumes of the *Life and Writings of George Washington*. The biography was published separately in 1838, and in 1839 in two volumes, the so-called "abridged edition." Subsequent editions were published by various printers/publishers through 1860. The biography was well received and brought praise from John Marshall, George Bancroft, Edward Everett, and William Prescott. Typical of their comments was this by Bancroft to Sparks upon receiving a copy of the separate edition of the "Life": "It is saying little to say your book should be in every American family; you have been the first to give the world a full length portrait of Washington, and I set the highest value alike on your larger picture and on this its miniature."

Sparks' work on the writings of George Washington was not without controversy, however. He was criticized in many circles for the editorial license taken with the prose of Washington's letters, which Sparks altered to conform to more acceptable grammar and phrasing, eliminating or altering certain of Washington's descriptive writings concerning prominent individuals. Sparks justified his editorial work by stating that Washington's letters were private writings, not intended for public exposure and that in the interests of "the dignity of history" he would not have wanted them exposed without proper correction. Even so, the controversy continues wherever Sparks is spoken of, and is often referred to today when similar adjustments are made in the release of private papers, correspondence, and other writings.

Washington Irving
(4/3/1783 — 11/28/1859)

Life of George Washington, by Washington Irving. New York, G.P. Putnam, 1855.

Washington Irving was born in New York on April 3, 1783, the week of the British cease fire that ended the Revolutionary War. His mother named him after George Washington, whom he met at the age of six in New York after Washington's inauguration as president in 1789. In the same year, due to an outbreak of yellow fever in Manhattan, he was sent to live with friends at Tarrytown in upstate New York. It was there he was exposed to local Dutch culture, legends, ghost stories, Sleepy Hollow, and the Catskills. He began writing in earnest at the age of nineteen, submitting commentaries to newspapers under the name of Jonathan Oldstyle, the first of many pseudonyms he would use. He travelled to Europe in 1804, financed by his brothers, and on his return two years later collaborated on publishing a literary magazine, *Salmagundi,* in which he first used the nickname "Gotham" for New York City. In 1809 he completed work on his first book *A History of New York from the Beginning of the World to the End of the Dutch Dynasty,* under the pseudonym Diedrich Knickerbocker, purportedly a Dutch historian, whose name became identified as a nickname for New Yorkers.

Irving spent the years from 1815 to 1832 in Europe, where he completed *The Sketch Book of Geoffrey Crayon, Gent.*, which contained the story "Rip Van Winkle" and published in the United States in installments and in London in two volumes, later to include the story "The Legend of Sleepy Hollow." He was invited by the American Minister to Spain, Alexander Everett, to travel to Madrid to research the consul's library of Spanish history. There Irving began work on several projects: *The Life and Voyages of Christopher Columbus*, *The Chronicles of the Conquest of Granada*, and *Voyages and Discoveries of the Companions of Columbus*.

Irving's career was both literary and political. He was appointed Secretary to the American Legation in London in 1829, and stayed on there until 1832 when he returned to the United States. Ten years later he was appointed Minister to Spain by President Tyler, at the urging of Secretary of State Daniel Webster. Irving spent four years in Spain before returning to his home, Sunnyside, to begin work on a revised edition of his works for the publisher George Putnam. Irving's habit was to work on several writing projects simultaneously, and he had begun work on a life of George Washington some time before settling back into New York, envisioning a multivolume biography that would be the crowning achievement of his life's work.

Realizing the amount of work a "Life of Washington" would require, Irving hired his nephew Pierre as full time assistant in 1854. Pierre would compile information and write preliminary chapters, as he had for the writing of *Astoria*. Irving planned his *Life of George Washington* as a thorough narrative history as opposed to the popular "life and letters" biographies of the type published by Jared Sparks, Bancroft and others. Irving's work relied on the latest published histories and on public documents, including Sparks' publication of Washington's correspondence. In addition, Irving consulted British and French writings on the Revolution, the *Journals of the Continental Congress*, Chief Justice Marshall's biography of Washington, the memoirs of Revolutionary War generals, and the *Annals of Congress*. Irving was of the belief that Washington was basically a public man, and stated in his preface to his biography that the story of America's independence and nationhood was indistinguishable from that of Washington's, who was the "principal actor."

Aware of the criticisms of Sparks and Marshall regarding their writing technique, Irving approached his *Life of George Washington* as a professional writer, paying attention to style and readability. Further, being aware of the pedestal upon which Washington rested, Irving tended to protect his subject from full exposure, refraining from telling all he had learned about Washington's petulance and irritability. The result is a well-researched, accessible biography that stays within the established trend, a complimentary narrative of a man of morals and unselfish commitment.

Early in 1855 Putnam released the first volume of Irving's *Life of George Washington*, which covered the period up to the American Revolution. The reviews were positive, and Putnam promised the public that volume two would be published in August and volume three in October, a schedule Irving was unable to meet. In fact volume two was not ready until Christmas, and proved to be a difficult volume to write, as it dealt with the Revolution requiring descriptions of battles and Washington's military leadership. As with the first volume, the second was highly praised, with Prescott writing that it portrayed Washington as a "flesh and blood" figure, and "one with whom we can have sympathy."

The third volume was published in July, 1856, covering the period from the encampment at Morristown through Washington's fortification of West Point. This volume is prefaced by Irving: "When the author commenced the publication of this work, he informed the publishers that he should probably complete it in three volumes... His theme has unexpectedly expanded under his pen, and he now lays his third volume before the public, with his task yet unaccomplished...To present a familiar and truthful picture of the Revolution and the personages concerned in it, required much detail and copious citations, that the scenes might be placed in a proper light, and the characters introduced might speak for themselves, and have space in which to play their parts."

It took Irving all of volume four, published in May 1857, to close out his narrative of the Revolution, ending with Washington's election to the presidency and the inauguration. In his preface to volume five, May 1859, Irving wrote: "The present volume completes a work to which the author had long looked forward as the crowning effort of his literary career...How far this, the last labor of his pen, may meet with general acceptation is with him a matter of hope rather than confidence...Grateful, however, for the kindly disposition which has greeted each successive volume, and with a profound sense of the indulgence he has experienced from the public through a long literary career...he resigns his last volume to its fate...." The accolades for Irving's completed work attested to Irving's standing in literary America, and to the copious research and narrative style of the biography.

The *Life of George Washington* proved to be Irving's last work. His health declined as winter approached, and he died in November 1859, at the age of 76.

Selected Bibliography

Adams, Herbert. *The Life and Writings of Jared Sparks*. Boston: Houghton, Mifflin & Co., 1893.

Armentrout, Donald. "Weems, Mason Locke," *Encyclopedia of the Enlightenment*, Kors, Alan, editor. Oxford University Press.

Beveridge, Albert. *The Life of John Marshall*. Boston: Houghton, Mifflin & Co., 1944.

Burstein, Andrew. *The Original Knickerbocker*. New York: Basic Books, 2007.

Harris, Christopher. *Public Lives, Private Virtues: Images of American Revolutionary War Heroes, 1782-1832*. New York: Garland Publishing, 2000.

Johnson, Paul. *A History of the American People*. New York: Harper Collins, 1997.

Jones, Brian. *Washington Irving, an American Original*. New York: Arcade Pub. Inc., 2008.

Sabin, Joseph. *A Dictionary of Books relating to America from its Discovery to the Present Time*. Mansfield: Martino Pub., 2002.

Weems, Douglas Andes. *History of the Weems Family*. Annapolis: Weems System of Navigation, 1945.

Wood, Gordon. *Revolutionary Characters*. New York: Penguin Press, 2006.

LaVergne, TN USA
25 February 2011

218030LV00001B/1/P

LU00055249523